PELICANS

LIVING WILD

Published by Creative Education and Creative Paperbacks
P.O. Box 227, Mankato, Minnesota 56002
Creative Education and Creative Paperbacks are imprints of The Creative Company
www.thecreativecompany.us

Design and production by Mary Herrmann
Art direction by Rita Marshall
Printed in China

Photographs by Creative Commons Wikimedia (Mike Baird/Flickr, CLPramod, Diego Delso, Manuel González Olaechea y Franco, Frank Schulenburg, Unknown, Frank Vassen/Flickr, Francesco Veronesi/Flickr, F.G. Waller-Fonds/ Karel van Mallery, Yuktijoshi24), Dreamstime (Alfotokunst, Andremichel, Mircea Bezergheanu, Donyanedomam, Fogen, Nicola Gordon, Attila Jandi, Jjjroy, Modfos, Peterll, Karunakaran Parameswaran Pillai, Jozef Sedmak, Theripper), Getty Images (Auscape/UIG), iStockphoto (A_Lein), Shutterstock (a9photo, A_Lein, attilavalentina, Tanja Bezuidenhout, Steve Bower, Catmando, jo Crebbin, Steffen Foerster, Arto Hakola, Ammit Jack, Eduard Kyslynskyy, Longjourneys, MarkVanDykePhotography, Nadezda Murmakova, MZPHOTO.CZ, Shahin Noyon, outcast85, Pecold, Peterson-Media, David Porras, taviphoto, Warren Price Photography, Wollertz)

Library of Congress Cataloging-in-Publication Data
Names: Gish, Melissa, author.
Title: Pelicans / Melissa Gish.
Series: Living wild.
Includes bibliographical references and index.
Summary: A look at pelicans, including their habitats, physical characteristics such as their flexible gular pouches, behaviors, relationships with humans, and their vulnerability to pollution in the world today.
Identifiers: LCCN 2016036684 / ISBN 978-1-60818-832-1 (hardcover) / ISBN 978-1-62832-435-8 (pbk) / ISBN 978-1-56660-880-0 (eBook)
Subjects: LCSH: Pelicans—Juvenile literature.
Classification: LCC QL696.P47 G57 2017 / DDC 598.4/3—dc23

CCSS: RI.5.1, 2, 3, 8; RST.6-8.1, 2, 5, 6, 8; RH.6-8.3, 4, 5, 6, 7, 8

First Edition HC 9 8 7 6 5 4 3 2 1
First Edition PBK 9 8 7 6 5 4 3 2 1

CREATIVE EDUCATION • CREATIVE PAPERBACKS

PELICANS

Melissa Gish

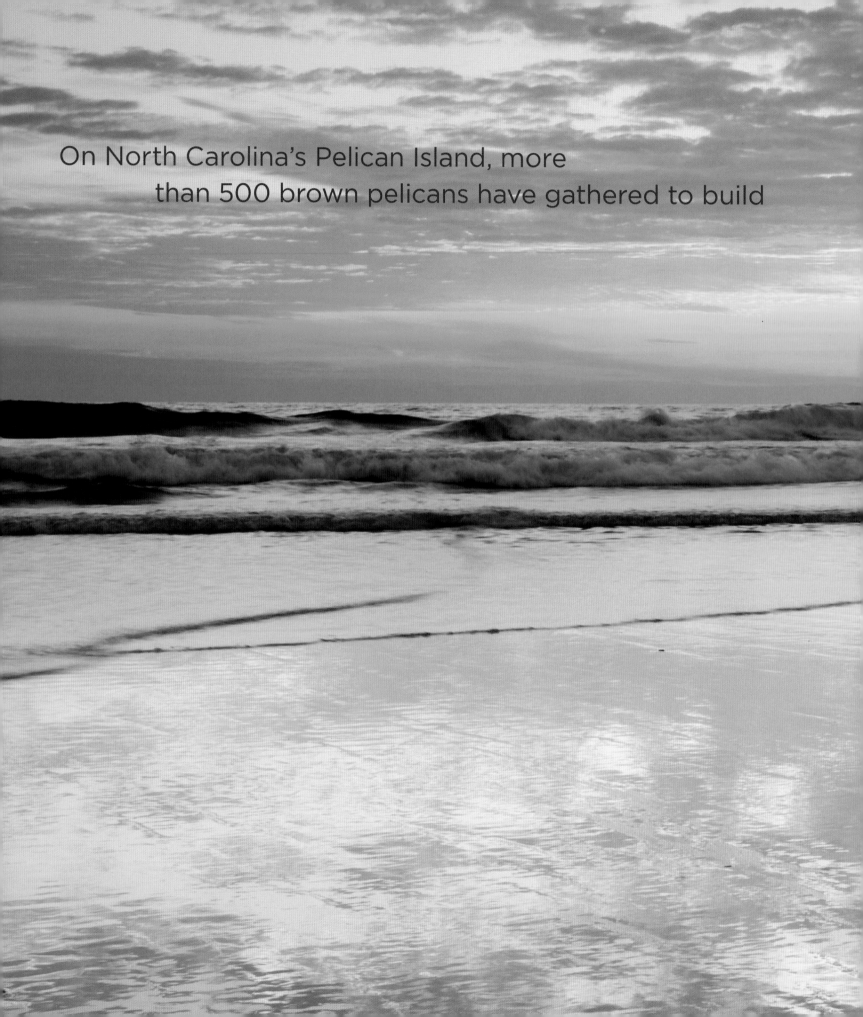

On North Carolina's Pelican Island, more
than 500 brown pelicans have gathered to build

nests and raise their young. The nests are crowded on the tiny, 20-acre (8.1 ha) island.

O n North Carolina's Pelican Island, more than 500 brown pelicans have gathered to build nests and raise their young. The nests are crowded on the tiny, 20-acre (8.1 ha) island. The pelicans stand shoulder-to-shoulder, squawking impatiently. For most of the birds, the time has come for their chicks to hatch. Constant cheeping has emanated from within the eggs for the last 48 hours. The chicks have been calling to their parents even before they

hatch, and their parents have called back. In this way, the family learns to recognize one another by sound. Gulls circle overhead, searching the nests below for unguarded eggs. The cheeping gets louder. Tiny bills poke holes in the eggshells, and the pale pink skin of the pelican chicks becomes visible. Excited parents squawk louder, greeting their hatchlings. By tomorrow, the island's population will nearly double with the arrival of hundreds of new baby pelicans.

WHERE IN THE WORLD THEY LIVE

■ **Dalmatian Pelican**
southeastern Europe through Asia

■ **Great White Pelican**
southeastern Europe to Myanmar and throughout Africa

■ **Spot-billed Pelican**
southern Pakistan, India, and Indonesia

■ **Pink-backed Pelican**
Africa and southern Arabia

■ **Australian Pelican**
Australia, New Guinea, and eastern Indonesia

■ **Peruvian Pelican**
northern Peru to central Chile

■ **Brown Pelican**
North and Central America, and the Galápagos Islands

■ **American White Pelican**
North America, Mexico, and Central America

The eight pelican species, divided into Old World and New World groups, range throughout the world in various watery habitats. Representative locations of wild populations of each species are indicated by the colored squares on the map.

SEABIRD SQUADRONS

P elicans are found on every continent except Antarctica. The name "pelican" is derived from the Greek word *pelekys*. The eight different species of pelican make up the family Pelecanidae. They are members of the order Pelecaniformes, which also includes families of herons and egrets, ibises and spoonbills, the shoebill, and the hamerkop. The latter two are the pelican's closest relatives. They are stork-like birds that share bill and flight characteristics with pelicans.

The largest pelican species, the Dalmatian pelican, is also one of the largest and heaviest birds on Earth. It averages 25 pounds (11.3 kg) and has a wingspan of more than 11 feet (3.4 m). The smallest pelican is the brown pelican. It rarely weighs more than 12 pounds (5.4 kg) and has an average wingspan of about 8 feet (2.4 m). Some pelicans exist solely in coastal habitats, while others live on inland lakes, marshes, and ponds. Pelicans can survive only where there are abundant fish, their main food source.

Pelicans are divided into two groups: Old World and New World pelicans. Old World pelicans are limited to the Eastern Hemisphere. New World pelicans are found

Unlike their pelican cousins, the much smaller, slenderer egrets do not have webbed feet.

The pink back and rump of a pink-backed pelican can be seen only when the bird's wings are spread wide.

in the Western Hemisphere. There are five Old World species. The great white pelican lives in shallow, warm lakes and swamps from southeastern Europe to Myanmar and throughout Africa. Named for its saddle of pale pink feathers, the pink-backed pelican lives in swamps, slow rivers, and shallow lakes in Africa and southern Arabia. The Dalmatian pelican is found in swamps and lakes from southeastern Europe through Asia. The spot-billed pelican prefers large lakes from southern Pakistan across India to Indonesia. The Australian pelican can be found near both inland and coastal waters of Australia and New Guinea as well as in eastern Indonesia.

New World pelicans include the American white pelican, which spends summers in lakes and swamps throughout North America and then **migrates** to Mexico and Central America during the winter. The Peruvian pelican lives on the west coast (and coastal islands) of South America, from northern Peru to central Chile. The five subspecies of brown pelican are divided by geographical habitat. The Caribbean brown pelican ranges along the eastern coasts of North and South America and the West Indies. The eastern brown pelican

In southwestern Africa, great white pelicans are known to eat the chicks and eggs of other water birds.

An abundant species, pink-backed pelicans live in colonies consisting of up to 500 pairs.

remains on the Atlantic coast from North Carolina to South America's Orinoco River basin. The California brown pelican lives on the Pacific coast from California to northern Peru. The Pacific brown pelican is found only from Colombia to northern Peru, and the Galápagos brown pelican is named for its island habitat.

Like all birds, pelicans are **warm-blooded**, feathered animals that walk on two feet and lay eggs. Pelicans' feathers, called plumage, range in color from white to gray to brown. Their bills also vary in color—from the Australian pelican's pale pink bill to the Peruvian pelican's bright orange bill to the brown pelican's rust-colored bill. Pelicans' bills are hooked at the tip so that the birds can hold on to slippery fish. The most striking characteristic of a pelican is its gular pouch. This bag of skin stretches from the bottom part of the bill, called the lower mandible, to the neck. A pelican uses its gular pouch like a fishing net to scoop up water and fish. The pouch can hold up to three gallons (11.4 l) of water. Contracting its tongue muscles, the pelican squeezes out the water in its pouch. Then it tilts its head back to swallow the captured fish whole. The pouch is also part of the pelican's cooling system. Pelicans

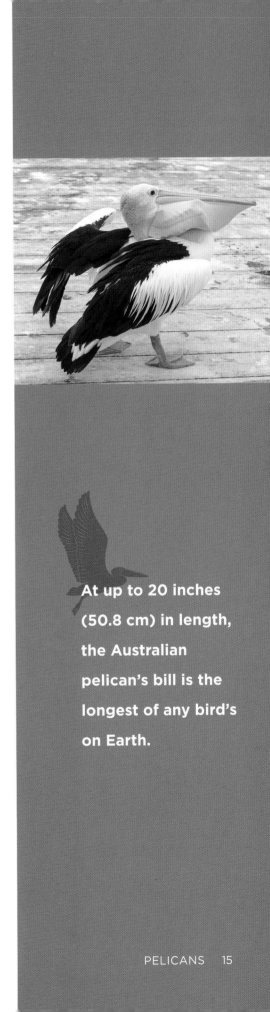

At up to 20 inches (50.8 cm) in length, the Australian pelican's bill is the longest of any bird's on Earth.

Through practice, pelicans learn that diving at angles between 60 and 90 degrees increases their target accuracy.

cannot sweat to alleviate heat. Similar to the way dogs pant to cool themselves, pelicans flutter their pouch—up to 250 times per minute—to release heat from their bodies.

Like many aquatic birds, pelicans are anisodactylous (*an-EYE-suh-DAK-til-us*), which means they have three toes that point forward and one that points backward. Pelicans' feet are webbed. Their toes are connected by a thin membrane that acts like a paddle, propelling the pelicans through the water as they search for food. Pelicans have sharp vision that helps them see schools of fish moving underwater.

Two pelican species plunge-dive for their food: Peruvian and brown pelicans fly high above the water. When they spot fish below, they dive headfirst into the water at speeds of up to 35 miles (56.3 km) per hour. The pelicans hit the water so hard that fish swimming as deep as six feet (1.8 m) under the surface are stunned, making them easier to catch. For a human, hitting the water at such a speed would be enough to break bones. Pelicans are protected from injury by a network of internal air sacs that cushions their organs and bones. The head and neck go underwater, but the air sacs help the body pop

The pelican folds up the webbing on its feet to fly and spreads out the webbing to swim.

immediately back out of the water. The air sacs also help pelicans stay afloat while resting.

Like their ancestors, modern birds have hollow bones, making them lightweight for flight. Wide wingspans enable pelicans to glide for great distances without pumping their wings. Pelicans fly low when the wind is blowing against them because wind is not as strong closer to the water. In open spaces, particularly over the sea, pelicans fly high, riding upward-moving currents of warm air that push them forward. By riding these currents, called thermals, pelicans can soar for great distances without flapping their wings.

Another way pelicans conserve energy is by flying in a V-shaped group called a squadron. The pelican in front creates an upward current of air with its wingtips. This upwash gives the pelicans following the lead bird a little boost. Squadron members take turns moving to the front of the V to share the burden of creating the upwash. In 2001, French **ecologist** Henri Weimerskirch put heart rate monitors on a squadron of pelicans. He found that birds at the back of the formation had lower heart rates than those toward the front, and they flapped their wings less often.

A pelican squadron is so named because it resembles the way that military aircraft move together in formation.

When they spot an abundant food source, pelicans flock together to engage in a feeding frenzy.

While pelicans eat mainly fish, some also eat frogs, snakes, and even other birds. When catching fish, a squadron of pelicans works cooperatively. Pelicans that feed from the water's surface often fly in a U-shape around a school of fish. They drive the fish toward shallow water by pounding their wingtips on the surface of the water. Plunge-diving pelicans may form a circle and drive fish into a tight school. Then the pelicans dive into the center of the school. Pelicans routinely fly more than 100 miles (161 km) a day seeking food. They usually stay close to shore but may travel as far as 40 miles (64.4 km) out to sea in search of fish. A pelican typically eats four to six pounds (1.8–2.7 kg) of fish per day.

Pelicans squawk, grunt, and hiss to communicate vocally. Pelicans also communicate with body language. Swinging the head from side to side and spreading the wings may communicate familiarity with other pelicans. Pelicans defending food or nests typically bow and sway their heads while grunting. Pelicans must preen often. Preening is a form of grooming that is vital to keeping feathers waterproofed and in good shape. Feathers have

Pelicans transfer oil from their uropygial (yoor-uh-PIDG-ee-ul) glands, at the base of the tail, to each feather.

While preening, a pelican will often raise its beak straight up in the air to clear its throat.

The endangered Dalmatian pelican is one of the world's heaviest flying birds.

The pelican's eyesight is so keen that it can spot fish swimming in the water while flying 65 feet (19.8 m) above.

tiny hooks called barbules that interlock to provide **insulation** from the cold. Regular preening keeps all the barbules hooked together. Pelicans also use their long bills to pull oil from a **gland** near their tail and spread it on their feathers. This oil waterproofs the feathers.

Pelicans are old enough to reproduce by age four or five. They do not mate for life, but they do mate with only one partner each year. Although some pelicans nest year round where food is abundant, for most pelicans, February, March, and April mark the height of nesting season. Pelicans nest in groups called colonies. Some colonies are small, with no more than 20 pairs. Others are enormous, with 500 pairs building nests so close together their edges touch. Pelicans seek out islands that offer protection from predators such as bobcats, wild dogs, and raccoons. During nesting season, these islands are usually shared with other birds such as egrets, herons, and cormorants. On islands with trees, pelicans may build nests of twigs and leaves. Where trees are sparse, pelicans will fashion nests on the ground by scraping out shallow depressions and filling them with scattered bits of leaves and brush.

About once every 10 years, roughly one-third of Australia's pelican population undertakes an incredible journey. From the eastern coast, Australian pelicans fly more than 600 miles (966 km) to the heart of South Australia's Lake Eyre. An empty lakebed, Lake Eyre is one of the hottest, driest places on the planet. Every decade or so, heavy rains flood the streams and rivers of southern Australia, which in turn pour into Lake Eyre, filling it to about 13 feet (4 m) deep. With the floodwaters come fish—

Scientists consider Australia's pelican migration to Lake Eyre one of nature's most enduring mysteries.

When pelicans catch food, they normally eat it right away, except when carrying it to their chicks.

lots of fish. About 100,000 pelicans make their way to Lake Eyre to feast, mate, and nest in relative safety.

All pelicans raise just one or two offspring per breeding season. The female lays one egg, and then a few days later she lays a second egg. Both parents take turns **incubating** the eggs for about a month. Rather than sit on the eggs as most birds do, pelicans hold the eggs under their feet. With just a few days left before hatching, the pelican chick inside the egg starts cheeping. This is so the parents learn to recognize their offspring's voice before it emerges from the egg. Chicks also have unique skin markings and eye color that help parents distinguish them from others in the colony.

Chicks are hatched blind and naked. They weigh two to four ounces (56.7–113 g), depending on species. The parents must constantly shade the chicks, because they cannot regulate their body temperature. A chick can die within five minutes if left unsheltered in the sun. Wispy feathers erupt on their bodies within two days, and by the time the chicks are two weeks old, they are covered with thick, fluffy down. At this age, they begin to drag themselves around the nest by their wings.

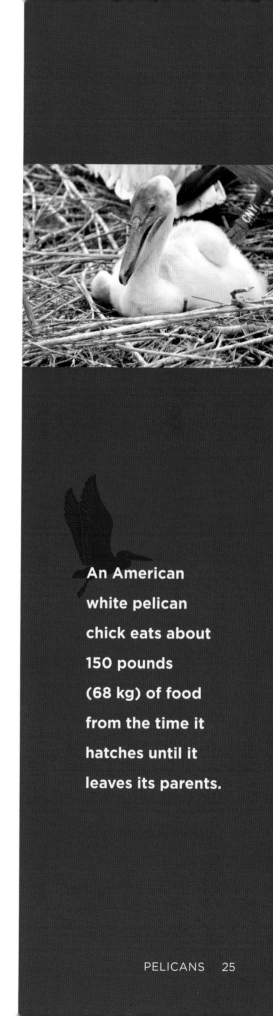

An American white pelican chick eats about 150 pounds (68 kg) of food from the time it hatches until it leaves its parents.

Young pelicans must strengthen their swimming and flying skills before joining their parents' squadron.

Each year, thousands of pelicans die from getting tangled in commercial fishing gear and sport-fishing hooks and lines.

At first, chicks feed up to 30 times a day, drinking liquid fish juice that dribbles from their parents' bills. After about two weeks, they move on to soft, predigested fish that is fed at least eight times a day. A chick must stick its entire head into its parent's throat to gobble up food. Where fish are plentiful, both pelican chicks usually survive. But where food is scarce, the stronger chick will often kill its weaker sibling. This enables the survivor to make the most of the limited food supply.

When chicks are about three weeks old, they leave their nests and gather in groups called crèches. Here they find relative safety in numbers. At about one month of age, the young pelicans' down has been replaced by feathers. They can swim and flap their wings, getting off the ground for moments at a time. They return to their nest just once a day to be fed by their parents. By the time they are two months old, the young pelicans have grown strong enough to fly and begin to catch their own fish. Within another month, the pelicans are mature enough to join a squadron and migrate with their parents to their regular feeding grounds.

Only one in three pelicans survives its first year. Young pelicans may not get enough food, or they may

become injured or sick. On ocean coasts, many pelicans fall prey to sharks that linger around schools of fish where pelicans feed. Pelicans that survive the hazards of life in the wild can live more than 15 years, and captive pelicans can live more than 20 years. Because pelicans have well-developed brains and good navigation skills, they remember where they were hatched and return there to raise chicks of their own. Even pelicans hatched in Australia's Lake Eyre remember—10 years later—how to get back to their nesting ground.

A parent pelican stores food in its pouch and in its throat, where chicks retrieve it.

A pelican statue symbolizing Jesus Christ stands in a Catholic church built in 14th-century Austria.

MAGICAL MYSTERY BIRDS

P elicans are important in the **mythology** and history of only a few **indigenous** peoples. The early Seri Indians inhabited western Mexico, from Sonora and around the Gulf of California to the Pacific coast. They witnessed countless migrating pelicans gathering in the warm waters around Mexico during the winter. Seri mythology describes the pelican as a magical bird that created the first island, which they called Pelican Island. The Seri people also made clothing and blankets from pelican hides.

The Nez Perce considered the pelican a magical bird, and seeing a pelican in a dream was a sign that a person had been granted spiritual powers. One of the most important Nez Perce Indian chiefs was named White Bird, but he was also called White Pelican. He was a shaman, or holy man, and a leader during the Nez Perce war with the U.S. Army. He had visions of his spirit animal, the American white pelican. The town of White Bird, Idaho, is named for him. It was the site of the Battle of White Bird Canyon in June 1877, a fight that occurred when the army fired on a group of Nez Perce who were seeking a truce. Guided

Nez Perce chief White Bird was guided in his decision-making by his spirit animal, the American white pelican.

Pelicans are among the many stone creatures that look down from high perches on France's Notre Dame Cathedral.

by his spirit animal, White Pelican later led more than a hundred people into Canada to escape army forces, which were sent to force the Nez Perce onto a reservation.

Pelicans are used as symbols in a variety of **cultures** around the world. In American Indian culture, **clans** are named after animals that were believed to provide special assistance or protection to the first clan members. The Ojibwa people of the Great Lakes region call their clan Pelican, or *Zhedeg*. On the other side of the globe, the Ngarrindjeri people of southern Australia have a legend about pelicans. The magpies told the pelicans that if they caught fish, the magpies would cook up the fish for the pelicans. Pleased with this arrangement, the pelicans caught many thukeri fish while the magpies built a fire. But when the fish were cooked, the magpies refused to share with the pelicans. The pelicans got angry and tossed the magpies into the ash of the fire. This turned the magpies black, just as they are today. Then the pelicans ate the fish, which turned their feathers white like the cooked fish.

The work of Jan Collaert II, a late 16th- and early 17th-century artist from Belgium, was included in a book called *Venationes Ferarum, Avium, Piscium (On*

Hunting Wild Beasts, Birds, Fish). Published in 1578, the book includes a scene of men on the bank of a river using pelicans to catch fish for them. In ancient times, it was a common practice to train pelicans and cormorants to capture fish and return the catch to land or to boats. Thousands of years ago, pelicans were used in Mesopotamia to pull fish from the Tigris and Euphrates rivers. While pelicans are no longer used in this way, in some parts of China, traditional fishermen still train cormorants from the time they are chicks to catch and deliver fish to their human masters.

Collaert and another engraver made a print of Indians Catch Fish Using Pelicans, *originally by Stradanus.*

8TH AUGUST 1804

The beak is a whiteish yellow the under part connected to a bladder like pouch, this pouch is connected to both sides of the lower beak and extends down on the under side of the neck and terminates in the stomach—this pouch is uncovered with feathers, and is formed [of] two skins the one on the inner and the other on the center side. A small quantity of flesh and strings of which the anamal has at pleasure the power of moving or drawing in such manner as to contract it at pleasure. In the present subject I measured this pouch and found its contents 5 gallons of water—

The feet are webbed large and of a yellow colour, it has four toes. The hinder toe is longer than in most aquatic fouls, the nails are black, not sharp and 1/2 an inch in length.

The plumage generally is white, the feathers are thin compared with the swan goose or most aquatick fouls and has but little or no down on the body. The upper part of the head is covered with black f[e]athe[r]s short, as far as the back part of the head—the yellow skin unfeathered extends back from the upper beak and opening of the mouth and comes to a point just behind the eye.

The large f[e]athers of the wings are of a deep black colour—the 1st & 2nd joint of [the wings] from the body above the same is covered with a second layer of white feathers which extend quite half the length of those large feathers of the wing—the thye is covered with feathers within a quarter of an inch of the knee.

From the journal of Meriwether Lewis (1774–1809)

In 1804, a team of American explorers led by Meriwether Lewis and William Clark were traveling down the Big Sioux River in Iowa when they came upon an astonishing sight. As Lewis described in his journal, a massive carpet of white feathers floated for a span of about 3 miles (4.8 km) and "pretty generally 60 or 70 yards [54.9–64 m] of the breadth of the river." The explorers were at first perplexed. But then, a little farther downriver, they saw the source of the feathers: molting American white pelicans. Like many aquatic birds, pelicans go through a period of about two weeks each year when all their feathers fall out at once. They cannot fly during this time as new feathers grow. According to Lewis's journal, the incredible number of pelicans could not even be estimated, for "they appeared to cover several acres of ground."

Louisiana is known as the Pelican State; the brown pelican is the state bird. It appears on Louisiana's state flag and seal and on the state's commemorative quarter, which was issued in 2002. When the National Basketball Association team the Charlotte Hornets relocated to New Orleans in 2002, it played only two seasons before Hurricane Katrina struck the Louisiana coast and

About 50 species of gulls exist, and most of them share their habitat with pelicans.

Gulls sometimes perch on pelicans' heads to steal fish from pelicans' mouths as they drain water from their pouches.

Pelicans regularly exercise and stretch their pouches, sometimes even turning them inside out over their breast.

devastated New Orleans. The team was forced to move temporarily, but when it returned, its owner decided to pay tribute to Louisiana's cultural heritage with a new name. In 2013, the team became the New Orleans Pelicans. Fans named a new mascot by voting on the team's website. On the opening night of the regular 2013 season, Pierre the Pelican was introduced to fans.

Pelicans have appeared in movies as animated characters and as real-life bird actors. The 2003 movie *Finding Nemo* features Nigel, a pelican who befriends Nemo and the other characters in the dentist's fish tank. He tells Nemo that his father is looking for him, prompting Nemo's escape from the tank. Later, Nigel helps Nemo's father and his forgetful friend Dory escape from the seagulls that want to eat them. In the film's ending credits, Nigel appears for the last time, utterly thrilled that Nemo is alive.

A real-life pelican movie star is Ricky, a great white pelican who played Rufus in the movies *Dolphin Tale* (2011) and *Dolphin Tale 2* (2014). Another pelican, Lucy, shared the role with Ricky. She died in 2015. Ricky lives at Clearwater Marine Aquarium in Florida, where he

serves as an ambassador for his species and other seabirds, spreading awareness of wildlife along America's coastal waters. The 2014 documentary film *Pelican Dreams* follows a starving California brown pelican that was rescued from the Golden Gate Bridge through to her rehabilitation and release back into the wild. The story of Gigi (named for Golden Gate) and another rescued pelican named Morro also includes a look at pelicans' annual migration and the many challenges these birds face in the wild.

Archaeopteryx *lived in what is now southern Germany during a time when Europe's climate was hot and humid.*

CHALLENGES TO SURVIVAL

A ll birds **evolved** from hollow-boned reptiles that existed millions of years ago. The link between reptiles and birds is the *Archaeopteryx*, a creature with feathered wings and reptilian teeth. It died out about 65 million years ago, but other birdlike creatures continued to evolve. One of the oldest pelican fossils dates to about 35 million years ago. It was found in the Ica Desert in western Peru, where the cool, dry climate helped preserve many fine details of the bird, including its skin. Klaus Hönninger, a Peruvian **paleontologist**, led the team that found the fossil in 2013. Still unnamed, the bird stood about 6.5 feet (2 m) tall.

In 2010, French paleontologist Antoine Louchart examined a much smaller fossilized pelican found in Luberon, a region in southeastern France. He determined that pelicans have changed very little since this 30-million-year-old bird existed. Prehistoric pelicans' bills and pouches are similar to those of modern pelicans. The bill, skull, and neck bones of the Luberon fossil closely resemble those of today's great white pelican. But this prehistoric bird was only about the size of the brown pelican. The fossilized

Ancient winged reptiles called pterosaurs are thought to have plunge-dived for fish like brown and Peruvian pelicans.

During mating season, pelicans' bills and pouches change color, displaying blue, pink, black, and yellow markings to attract mates.

bill is about 12 inches (30.5 cm) long, and the wing bones indicate the bird's wingspan was about 6.5 feet (2 m).

While most pelican species are either holding steady or increasing their numbers thanks to conservation efforts, the Dalmatian and spot-billed pelicans are in trouble. The International Union for Conservation of Nature (IUCN) lists the Dalmatian pelican as a vulnerable species, which means it is likely to become endangered unless changes are made to improve its chances of survival. Fewer than 10,000 mature individuals are believed to exist.

Today's engineering technologies allow rugged and swampy coastlines to be developed for human use. Buildings now surround the Mediterranean lagoons in Albania and Turkey where generations of Dalmatian pelicans once nested. In East Asia, urban development and increased tourism disturb nesting sites. Pelicans are also used in traditional folk medicines—in China and Mongolia, young pelicans are killed for their oily fat, and adult pelicans are killed for their bills. Also, increased human populations have led to the presence of more power lines, which pelicans frequently strike. And throughout the Dalmatian pelican's range, water pollution threatens the health of entire colonies.

Pelicans have powerful breast muscles made up of rope-like fibers that stiffen to lift the weight of their wings.

Pelicans use their webbed feet to race across the water's surface, gathering enough speed to take to the air.

The spot-billed pelican is listed by the IUCN as near threatened. The draining of wetlands and cutting of trees to expand urban areas leave the birds with little habitat suitable for nesting and raising young. Their feeding sites have been destroyed by chemical runoff from agriculture and the development of power stations that contaminate the water. Overfishing of species that pelicans need to survive has also contributed to the spot-billed pelican's decline.

A number of governments are addressing the plight of the Dalmatian and spot-billed pelicans. European nations such as Greece, Bulgaria, and Romania have instituted plans to reduce threats to the Dalmatian pelican by dismantling power lines and burying electrical cables. These countries are also building artificial nesting platforms and floating rafts. And they are increasing the number of law enforcement officers in areas where **poaching** is problematic. In Asia, the governments of Sri Lanka and Cambodia have committed to saving the spot-billed pelican. They have established protected areas for the birds as well as programs that educate citizens about environmental sustainability. In addition, programs are being developed to reduce the use of chemical pesticides in areas inhabited by aquatic birds.

On the other side of the world, not long ago, the brown pelican fell victim to many of the same threats its Old World cousins now face. Like many wild birds, millions of pelicans were slaughtered in the late 1800s when it became popular to decorate women's hats with bird feathers. For decades, brown pelicans were persecuted. Only in Florida did they find some relative safety.

A man named Paul Kroegel witnessed the decline of brown pelicans along Florida's east coast. He made it his mission to protect a small island in the Indian River Lagoon where brown pelicans nested. Kroegel carried a gun and chased off anyone who came near the island. He also went to

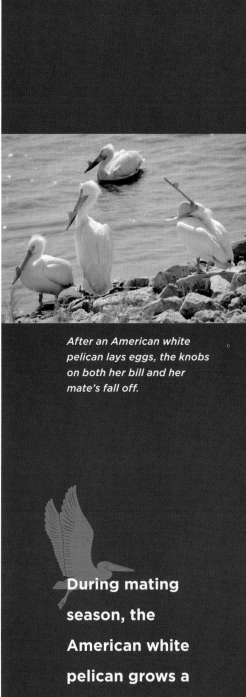

After an American white pelican lays eggs, the knobs on both her bill and her mate's fall off.

During mating season, the American white pelican grows a two-inch (5.1 cm) knob, or horn, on the top of its bill.

To keep its bill from hitting the ground while it sleeps, a pelican turns its head 180 degrees and lays its bill across its back.

the state government to ask for help. In 1901, Florida passed a law protecting non-game birds. But people continued to kill pelicans, so Kroegel went to the nation's capital to see president Theodore Roosevelt. A lover of wildlife, Roosevelt listened to Kroegel. In 1903, Roosevelt established Pelican Island National Wildlife Refuge. Game wardens were assigned to assist Kroegel in protecting the pelicans. Soon, the pelican population in Florida began to increase.

But 40 years later, the brown pelican faced a more insidious threat. After World War II, a chemical called **DDT** was introduced in America and many other countries as a pesticide. It polluted the soil and water. Birds ingested DDT-laced water and fish, which caused the shells of their eggs to be very thin. When the birds incubated their eggs, the shells would break. This led to plummeting populations of many bird species—including pelicans. By 1970, fewer than 1,000 pairs of brown pelicans existed.

When the public realized the effects of DDT and other chemicals, environmental awareness grew. In 1972, DDT was banned, and contaminated areas were cleaned up. Since then, the brown pelican population has increased by more than 700 percent. However, efforts to protect brown pelicans

must persist as threats from human activity continue.

The 2010 BP Deepwater Horizon oil spill discharged 210 million gallons (795 million l) of oil into the Gulf of Mexico. Nearly 2 million gallons (7.6 million l) of chemicals were dumped into the Gulf as part of the cleanup efforts. One of the worst environmental disasters in recent history, the spill affected millions of animals—including pelicans. Twelve percent of the brown pelican population was wiped out by the spill. Oil-covered pelicans became a global symbol for environmental responsibility. Pelicans around the world continue to struggle toward recovery, but sustained conservation measures can help these fascinating birds survive in a world filled with environmental challenges.

Unlike most land-dwelling birds of their size, pelicans are social, living in flocks and nesting in colonies.

ANIMAL TALE: THE PELICAN AND THE GULLS

The pelican may appear awkward on land, but it is a skilled fisher. Its relationship with crafty gulls is certainly not a friendly one. This folk tale from Louisiana's coastal heritage tells why the pelican feeds its young in such a unique way.

Long ago, when the pelican was new to the world, it was a bit clumsy. With short legs, broad wings, and a long, pouched bill, it often stumbled and tripped over itself. Such a body would take some getting used to. About the same time, the gulls came into being. They were very proud of their sleek appearance and often laughed at the pelican.

"Pelican is so awkward," the gulls said. "She must be very stupid. We will play a trick on her." So the gulls went to the pelican and told her about a marvelous school of anchovies swimming near shore. "You should go catch them," they told her. "We will help you."

"Oh, thank you," the pelican replied. She flapped her broad wings and, after a few tries, rose into the air and flew toward the sea.

The gulls followed as the pelican dove into the water and came up with a mouthful of delicious broad-striped anchovies. Still not used to her enormous pouch, the pelican was having some trouble getting the water to drain out.

"Just open your mouth," the gulls called, "we'll help you." When the pelican opened her mouth, the gulls swooped down and reached their heads into her pouch. In a flash, they gobbled up all of the anchovies.

The good-natured pelican shrugged, deciding that such misunderstandings sometimes happen among friends. For months, however, the gulls continued to steal fish from the pelican's pouch, each time assuring her that they were helping.

"Stupid pelican," the gulls chattered among themselves. "She doesn't even realize that we are not friends."

Soon it was time for the pelican to lay eggs. Her nest was crude, for she had never constructed one before. The gulls were very critical. "Stupid pelican," they said to one another. "She will probably crush her eggs or trample her babies."

But the pelican did not crush her eggs, nor did she trample her babies. In her nest, she hatched two little pelican chicks. She hurried out to sea to catch food for her babies. With much practice, she had become quite skilled and much less clumsy. But every time she came up with a mouthful of delicious anchovies or herring, the gulls were right there to "help" the pelican with her catch.

Finally, desperate to feed her chicks, the pelican quickly swallowed the fish, leaving the gulls nothing to take. Back at her nest, the pelican sat down and opened her mouth. Her chicks reached into her pouch but found no food. They reached farther into her mouth, but still, they found no fish. Then they poked their heads down her throat. There they found their meal, hidden deep in her gullet where the gulls had not seen it.

The gulls discovered that the pelican was not so stupid after all. She was simply too trusting. To this day, gulls try to steal food from the pelican's pouch. And this is why pelicans must carry food to their young hidden deep in their gullet.

GLOSSARY

clans – groups of interrelated families

cultures – particular groups in a society that share behaviors and characteristics that are accepted as normal by that group

DDT – a chemical compound used to kill pest insects that was later found to cause health problems in people who lived in the environments where it was used

ecologist – a person who studies the relationships of organisms living together in an environment

evolved – gradually developed into a new form

gland – an organ in a human or animal body that produces a chemical substance used by other parts of the body

incubating – keeping an egg warm and protected until it is time for it to hatch

indigenous – originating in a particular region or country

insulation – the state of being protected from the loss of heat

migrates – undertakes a regular, seasonal journey from one place to another and then back again

mythology – a collection of myths, or popular, traditional beliefs or stories that explain how something came to be or that are associated with a person or thing

paleontologist – a scientist who studies fossils of animals, plants, and other organisms that existed long ago

poaching – hunting protected species of wild animals, even though doing so is against the law

warm-blooded – maintaining a relatively constant body temperature that is usually warmer than the surroundings

SELECTED BIBLIOGRAPHY

Alderton, David. *The Complete Illustrated Encyclopedia of Birds of the World*. Leicestershire, UK: Lorenz Books, 2012.

ARKive. "Dalmatian pelican (*Pelecanus crispus*)." http://www.arkive.org/dalmatian-pelican/pelecanus-crispus.

Brazil, Mark. *Birds of East Asia: China, Taiwan, Korea, Japan, and Russia*. Princeton, N.J.: Princeton University Press, 2009.

Bright, Michael, Kate Fulton, and Sam Chung. "Outback Pelicans," *Nature*, season 29, episode 3. DVD. Directed by Susan McMillan. Sydney, Australia: Tindale Road Films, 2011.

National Geographic. "Pelican: *Pelecanus*." http://animals.nationalgeographic.com/animals/birds/pelican/.

San Diego Zoo Animals & Plants. "Pelican." http://animals.sandiegozoo.org/animals/pelican.

Note: Every effort has been made to ensure that any websites listed above were active at the time of publication. However, because of the nature of the Internet, it is impossible to guarantee that these sites will remain active indefinitely or that their contents will not be altered.

Pelicans face many challenges, from water pollution and habitat loss to increased instances of severe weather.

INDEX